The workshop

CONTENTS

The workshop

Bob makes guitars.

He has lots of tools in his workshop.

Hammers

There are lots of different hammers.

Hammers are for hitting things.
Bob uses a hammer to knock in nails.

Saws

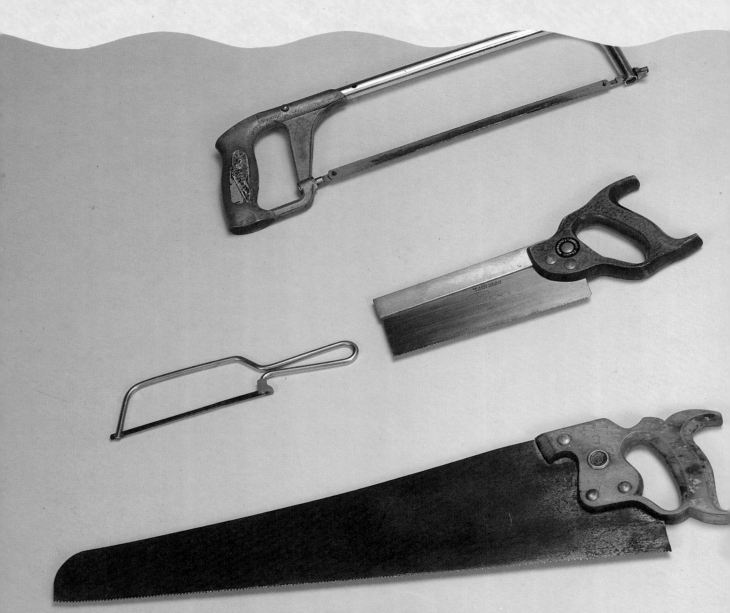

There are lots of different saws.

Saws are for cutting things.
Bob uses different saws
to cut wood and metal.

electric saw

tenon saw

junior hacksaw

Drills

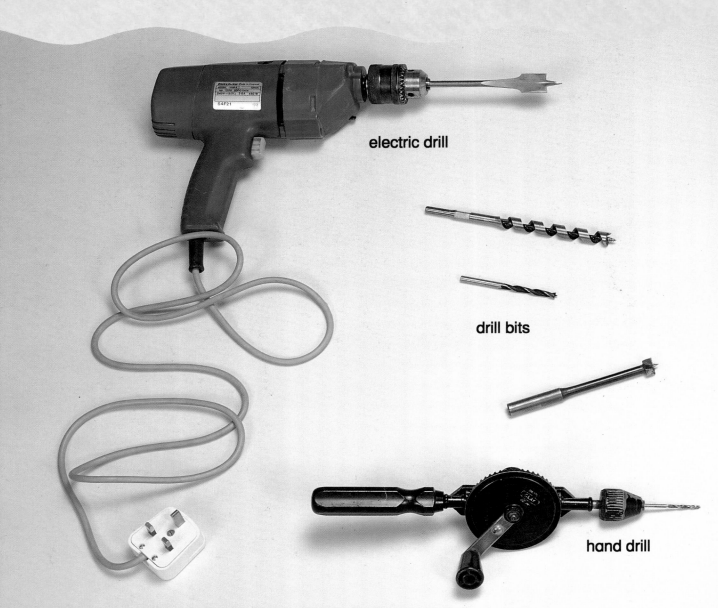

electric drill

drill bits

hand drill

There are lots of different drills.

Bob turns a drill to make a hole.

Chisels and planes

chisels

planes

There are chisels and planes.

Bob smooths
the wood
with a plane.

He knocks a
chisel into the wood.

Glue

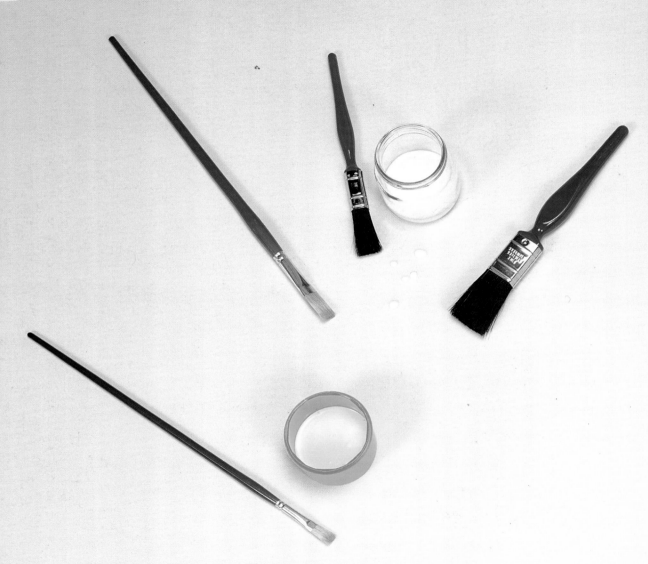

There are glue pots and brushes.

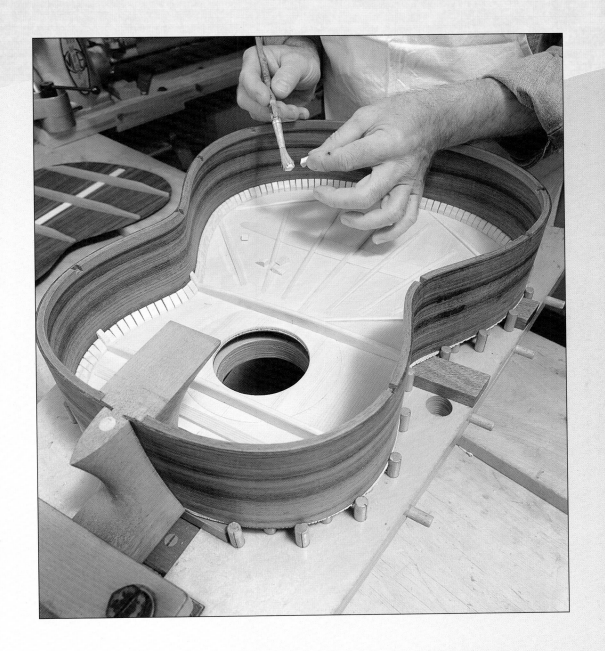

Bob sticks the wood together with glue.

How a guitar is made

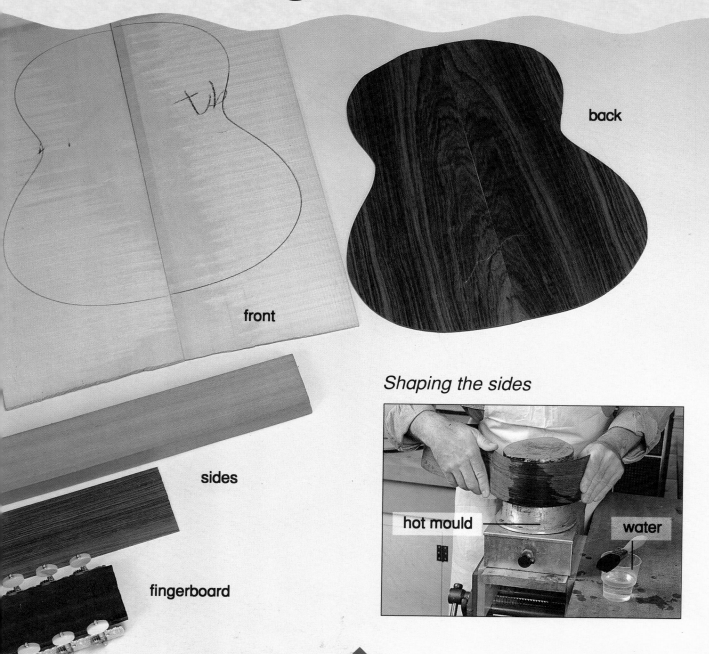

back

front

sides

fingerboard

Shaping the sides

hot mould

water

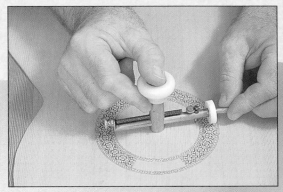

Making the hole

Putting the guitar together

The finished
guitar

Tuning the strings

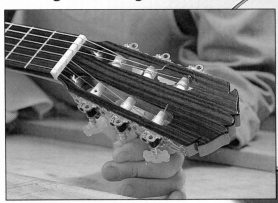

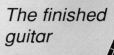

Index